To Clear a Static Field

To Clear a Static Field

P. J. HOLLIDAY

RESOURCE *Publications* • Eugene, Oregon

TO CLEAR A STATIC FIELD

Resource Publications
An Imprint of Wipf and Stock Publishers
199 W. 8th Ave., Suite 3
Eugene, OR 97401

www.wipfandstock.com

PAPERBACK ISBN: 978-1-6667-0754-0
HARDCOVER ISBN: 978-1-6667-0755-7
EBOOK ISBN: 978-1-6667-0756-4

07/01/21

For my family

". . .whatever
returns from oblivion returns
to find a voice."
—Louise Gluick, *The Wild Iris*

"Some/stories within us have been unfolding for years, others
are trembling with fresh life. . ."
—Joy Harjo, *Conflict Resolution for Holy Beings*

Contents

Impartation | 1

Part 1.

Someday a Son | 5
I Discovered My Father | 6
I Asked for a Little Yellow | 9
Level with Me | 10
Field in a Drought | 12
Consider the Lilies | 14
To Clear a Static Field | 15
The walls within me shake | 16
The Years I Prayed About Anxiety | 17
I tried to tell you | 18
Your Dad is Done Here | 19
Not Every Sunday in Church is Earth Shattering | 23
I am myself today   divine drawing | 24
Open Window | 25
The magnolias are about to bloom | 26
Wild Flower Arrangement | 27
Daydreaming | 28
Mantra | 29
Meditation | 31
To Earth We Return | 32
I Dream When I'm Rested | 33
Comforter | 34

Part 2.

I won't be wronged and feel nothing | 37

Men beat their chests | 38

Melancholy | 39

You don't think of us | 41

The fathers of this country exploit their children | 42

Family Passed | 43

Shelby says she lost her mother before the cancer | 46

At the House I Gather Things | 47

Conception | 48

My mother and I sat on the edge of the sofa | 49

I think about death too often | 50

Foreshadow | 51

Our Case Before the Court | 52

Geminis | 54

A month after the accident | 56

I can't breathe with you in the room | 57

I know what you're doing. You're becoming a moth | 59

I keep looking | 60

I Heard My Brother's Voice | 61

Origins of Healing | 62

I couldn't tell you about the accident | 63

The New Beatitudes | 65

Happiness Is | 66

The months before the baby comes are oddly still | 67

I find comfort in something | 68

Acknowledgments

I am deeply grateful to the many people who critiqued, encouraged, and championed my first book of poems. Thank you to my mentors at Regis University, particularly Eric Baus who helped me through my final drafts and the publishing process. I am forever grateful for your guidance. Allissa Hertz, my comrade in all things literary, this book would not exist without you. Thank you to my husband who gave me space to write and deliver eight drafts. To my undergrad mentors, Martha Serpas and Laurie Clements-Lambeth, thank you so much for teaching me to write a book and believing I could. Thank you, David Hicks, who's teasing of my elevator pitch led me to rewrite and produce a proper book proposal. And to Jesus, for bringing me through it all.

Impartation

It wasn't easy
to stand under the weight
of those pictures.

I held the world steady
as it spun out of order.

Were they real?
Were they actually here in this house?

In the empty rooms
I shouted,
my mouth corners
unable to hold the words
which fell from me
as my mind
began to loosen.

This is what it is
for those without hope.
For those who don't know
the other side of death
is meant for them.

Go and tell my people.

Part 1.

Someday a Son

That dream fueled a tight pull between two people once connected.
 I knew you before the sun held its light against your blond hair.
I heard your name echoed in my mind. A spring of vowels
coming up to earth through a hole in the garden.

A birth opened my body the morning after. Showed an edge to my femininity,
a place lying quiet in the mists of sleep. I welcome the effect of a blind spot taking over.
Fear says I'm not the right person. Says I can't see the heartbreak instore

to give my husband an heir, watch him live by his name.

I Discovered My Father

1.

Living inside me, imagined,
faint monogram. He wore
pearl snap shirts to go out
at night, a dingy box of
cigarettes stuck from his front
pocket. He called me back
to the house when
I wandered into wilderness.
The woods thickened,
his voice guided my steps
in darkness as sunlight
diminished into faint outlines
of trees around me.

2.

I hesitated, lost balance
looking down a cliff.
Rocks marbled together,
crystals appeared to
breathe in sunlight. I
concentrated on the horizon
line which stayed in place.

Once you're consumed
with falling, the body wants
to stop moving forward,
senses danger in its midst.
I spoke to my mind, sung
psalms into the marrow
of my bones. Pulled away
from what wasn't really
happening.

3.

I used to take it personal
when my father didn't call
on my birthday.
He attempted no effort
to light candles on top
of homemade cakes or lift
me to his shoulders
knowing the weight
of my body as I saw
from the height of his
            unobstructed view.

These days he's grown thin,
symptom of neglect and diabetes.
The stories of his drunken father
who chased him from home
behind a shotgun was an extreme
response to disciplining children.

Family can be punishment,
hesitations that sense danger.
I don't trouble him with bitterness
when he comes over for money
or explain the anxiety I traded
for absence. Deficiency
is just a hole to fill,
forgiveness
that does its own healing.

"The righteous will flourish . . .
they will grow like a cedar of
Lebanon."—Psalm 92:12 (NIV)

I Asked for a Little Yellow

                    in moonlight,
held out for clouds to move past
a portion of me
        left behind to hold the door.

I admire those able to
                morph
become the cedar tree.
The cool wind stabilizes
the middle of the garden.
        I let it chase me
        where the cracked fountain centers the earth.

Counting back from ten
        I inhale strands of lemongrass

        as leaves
            struggle against themselves.

Even trees are prone to panic.

Level with Me

A lover here, a father there,
each his own delicate place in my body.

What would have been different

had they understood the value
of what was cast aside?

I am covered

in deep mahogany,
bruises for all the

carelessness. When I say *I'm yours*,

I mean I will let the skin
that touched your skin
rest on me.

The shower rinses our closeness
knowing I must, again, wait
for your call on the weekend.

I didn't ask for this
internal struggle with family.

I was born with a need
for a father, a lover,

and deserve to be filled, too.

Wind that comes in one direction
and flees from you in seven.

Field in a Drought

When you stop trying, do you lose
your place in line, the effort put in?

The lady in my dream smiled —
You're doing better than you think you are.

The weight of what I'd been saying
lost its power, or my faith in it.

I've turned two vocal cords
into closed gates and nothing

passes without vetting. My heart
has been disappointed lately,

disillusioned because what used to work
doesn't anymore.

I am prepared for this, a different
way to view the field.

You never get the same experience twice.
There's always something else

blowing in the wind. It used to be
refinery smoke, now its word shaped

clouds, little clues for you to follow.

Consider the Lilies

(For Sam)

I can be strong for you.
I can pull the car over and wait
on you to finish crying. I can
pray and remember all the verses
I forget for myself. *I can
do all things*, I used to say.
I've grown quiet in the long wait
for wholeness, as if being whole
is meant for some time in the future.
The ground is damp from fresh rain.
Your neck, the stem of a lily,
stretches to the sun. Your eyes bloom
open and the green in them lightens.
At Target, we talk about your fears.
I hug your shoulders and listen to what
you're saying. It's been good for me too.

To Clear a Static Field

The old television had bulbs inside.

    It took time
           to clear a static field

time   to develop a feel
           for the switch.

Pliers were used to repair
           a mind separate   from itself

a voice bent behind silver
 distortions,
tremors in the throat.

Window light appears—
           a warm hand on the head,
     new life
beyond clouds and interruption.

    The screen inhales,
           recalls a last channel,
two blinking eyes
          opened   in the sun.

The walls within me   shake
while we talk regular things
I am used to
     the scrupulous sun
drying the ground
weakening roots
from time to time   I manage
clear speech   manage to think
I can perform this well
simple talk
speak/breathe/speak.

The Years I Prayed About Anxiety

I asked you to come for me, LORD.
You heard
    my voice in the whirlwind,
        allowed it to spin across my acres.

My house stands
    on pier and beam
    its ankles give way beneath me.
Where is the light
    promised?
The sun giving its own
    body
    to its brothers?

I tried to tell you
what is hard for me to say.
The dried grass in the yard is sad
it touched your ankle   enticed you to stay
I don't know what to do   when you call and hang up
when you leave home   for something wild
I know you've been depressed
but I was already yours   when you left
I was already a girl   in love with her father
and I would haunt you like a shadow
the rest of your days.

Your Dad is Done Here

Stay,
        don't
                leave

for the other side.

Don't tell me

            you're ready

 I'm not.

I dreamt of you
        dying,

tired
        by life.

It was
        all you could do
        to stay.

The hairs
            on my arm
        stick up,
become cold.

I don't want to watch you

        bury
        yourself
in dry
        dirt and clay

underneath

        an array of lilies

white as sun

        reflected
        on an old

window.

******

I'm not happy about it, but how do I argue?

        You have no quality
        of life here.

The grass isn't mowed. It sways around my ankles.

Remember smoking that joint with me

        Nothing that bad
        happens to you twice,
        you'd say.

Sometimes there was wisdom

exhaled like smoke from your mouth.

Everything was sad for us.
I believe
you chose it,

made your bed
                of matches and Marlboro reds.

I forced my way into the house
                when I was old enough
                to drive there.

You didn't argue,
                though you were never home for dinner.

                Our thing was Dairy Queen
                because we didn't own
                a family table.

Still, we're friends.

                Your diabetes scares me.

I would hold my breath

if it would keep you

 intact.

I look at time like numbers skipped over a lake of numbers.

Not Every Sunday in Church is Earth Shattering

You contain   space   for only

so

much

/worry/

/fear/

indignation when the car driver sees you
        and though you're pregnant
doesn't let you cross the road first.

The worship leader cries as she sings,
lays her body against the altar.

My husband doesn't rush me
out of church today.

I am grateful
        for hands and the room around me
    unable to move   because of peace.

I am myself today   divine drawing
thought in the mind of one writing herself
a story

I am   road ragey
brake checking the erratic car behind me
scared   of his gun
I'm not going to cry in this movie
beside this woman
who wouldn't understand
it's about my father

I am finite mathematical   a sphere of my own dimensions.

Open Window

I cannot speak—
let me write you

of the glory
of opened windows,

little hamlets
with church on the outside,

forest green arrangements,
sun for when it's cold

and nakedness is unavoidable.

The little arch in the branch,
a bed to sleep in

a womb to place your hands.

Leaves collect in the garden,
know their indentations.

The wind comes to push
on the old, brown fragments,

but first, the orange,
a little song at the end.

The magnolias are about to bloom
I don't like them   tight claws
coming out of leaves that propel them
                    I don't dare call them   dandelion
for fear they might   break   apart
                come through a screen door
I long to see them less   irritated with blooming
long to see
              the white irrigated petals
untuck their folded arms
long to smell their brazen pollen
            irresistible powdered petals

that know in beauty

                    they're up against nothing.

Wild Flower Arrangement

I won't look for you
in the crowd

or turn to see you smile
as I bring out my newborn.

I don't have to.

I have another father
watching me dance.

Morning glories,

sweet magnolias
pushed into bloom.

I'm not as alone as I thought.

I am comforted
by marigolds,

orange sponge petals.

Fathers come from fathers.
There are many I belong to

and one.

Daydreaming

I emerged from thought
seeing my teacher wave her hands
slowly in front of the class   *PeeeJaaay*
she whispered
wanting me to pay attention
not to miss this thing
a book she held open
with one hand.

Mantra

To take your mind off pain
someone might break
your other finger,
transfer power,
change guards at the gate.

I'd cheat pain,
disregard
knowing the first or
second wound.

My atmosphere would
be unfiltered,
flat, unruly.

I would barter peace,
stand for nothing,
fulfill nothing.

I'd never know the taste
of earned fruit,
pomegranate seeds
spit from the rind.

But because of the garden,
I honor the universe,

plow the soil,
plant seeds,
prune,

a constant practice,
participation in the fields.

Meditation

I remember it as a kid,
in the car on the left side,
skimming over the earth,
completely vacant.
For a moment
I took cover,
only to be reminded
that grass blades
slow along the median
when I focus.

To Earth We Return

July is too warm to spread your father's ashes.
He was never one to be contained.
Autumn signals an end. Birch tree's
mute their vibrant reds. Cool winds
shift the leaves, detach—In the end,
my father carried on inside the house,
content with television, videos and other
man-made comforts. His heart closed
to me, vines grew over the front door.
To him life was a way back, a return.
He sees now the earth is wild
enough to take him in.

I Dream When I'm Rested

I dreamt of being
 happy.
I dreamt I rode that horse along the edge
              of the water.
I dreamt I wore no restrictive harness.

Water foams at the horse's legs.
We gain speed and turn sharply.

          I feel its smooth hair
              smell salt crest at its side
                  concede to its mood.

Over the horse's long neck, I pry my eyes open

As we're born together
And dream of nothing else.

Comforter

You are   the short distance to leave this place
the distance across town
                 beside me
when she said   my father wasn't meant to be a father

     I find comfort I did not have then
crying under her arm

a little girl
who wanted her daddy.

Part 2.

I won't be wronged and feel nothing
 pursue nothing
there is sickness in American industry
I will not let their names lie silent under the oak trees of Rosewood
Cemetery
the small characters we used to write epitaphs
 a body   a story
do not deny my voice
I am no longer choking on my pillow
weeping at my bedside
screaming into the open sky of the neighborhood we lived in

 I loved them.

                    That is what you should fear.

Men beat their chests
           on top of buildings

roam the halls of   court   in the ears of those
who pull levers.

I am no small thing.

I can feel engines steal
           into grassy medians,

my legs unable to press deep into loose breaks,

the child's breath against my shoulder,
the angel
    who makes a ring in the grass.

Melancholy

I ask friends to console me
lying on the carpet in an empty house
begging on the phone for someone.
I am withered, dissolving
like the potato chips I ate for breakfast,
testing their weight in my hands.
I saw the abyss
by the stove,
the flatness of trauma,
the open field like static before me.
It hums. It's white noise, the phone line disconnecting.

This is a book of recalled vehicles.

You don't think of us
now that the courtroom doors are shut.
I am a pebble
 under your pillow
you have been hurricanes
in my house
my hand is a microphone
        a balled fist
my siblings speak into.

The fathers of this country exploit their children
over the blueprints of city maps.
I've trembled in fear.
They left a legacy of violence,
scraped the concrete roads in America.
Against my will,
my hands shifted the car in drive
but it chose Adam in October   on a Tuesday.

Family Passed

Holding her hand
wrapped in cellophane
to keep the skin together
Danielle watched her mother die

In great agony
she took her brother
by the bedside
the two of them   their mother's silence

They pulled cables from the wall
her breath exited   *relief*

It was a year after my family passed.
A year after all I ever saw
was death anymore
Kelly   Melanie   Uncle Harry   Adam and the kids

am I cursed
a friend of mine asked
have you come to be my friend
to prepare me to lose

I hope not   I said

in that moment I realized

the preciousness of life
or its lack

and needed to know which.

PJ, will you get some things from the house?

Shelby says she lost her mother before the cancer.
Bitterness
staged
in her heart,
grew tentacles,
attached to her breasts.

She watched her mother wither,
the frailty of bone,
a spec of light.

At the House I Gather Things

Forgive me
if I can't stand
to have you over
with my dead brothers here,
their clothes   papers in a waste bin.
I wrote my name on a dresser
I gave to my brother
who wrote his name beside it.

I need to be alone
before for the funeral,
in the house with their things.
Why do materials make us feel close to the ones we've lost?
Why does Shelby need all her mother's furniture?
I took Isaac's SpongeBob toothbrush
Rachel's comb
a few strands   of her brown hair.

Conception

Who was in the car?
I scream into the phone
My mother's voice hesitates

PJ, there were no survivors.

The carpet becomes wet.
I'm coming to you
I scream again
She begs me not to drive

and she is right. I can't see a thing on the road.

My mother and I sat on the edge of the sofa. *If anything ever*
happened to any of you, I don't know what I'd do.
Her eyes looked away to the picture of the desert on the wall across
us.
She was beyond it, quietly begging god not to take her children.
Years would pass and many average days. Her voice trembled with
news
on the phone. *For I know the plans you have for me*
repeating over and over in the cave of her mouth.

I think about death too often
not to think of God.

I am keenly aware something floats in my room

in the stillness of curtains when the air conditioner turns off.
I rub my pillow corner, tuck it close behind my neck.

My husband stays asleep unless it's his turn
to think of other dimensions.

In church, my pastor says God hides in the darkness.

I find him here: a grassy medium

my eyes toward heaven

wondering where

where have they gone from me?

Foreshadow

The lines on my palms say nothing of this
but a prophet predicted the trauma,
ashes along the highway
empty boxes in the ground.
They are not there.
They do not sleep.
I live among the dead.
I feel their eyes watch me,
sometimes turn to see who is there.
My dreams are alive with their celebrations,
the kids dance in our old house
as if to tell me somehow, we've won.
Somehow   they always knew this.

Our Case Before the Court

I held the court's decision

       in the middle of my chest
   the edges of my ear
       where it burned

These men and their money
       the government they mock
a business has rights to commit fraud
   delegate to justices
       what constitutes a law

you have no standing, says the court

but we are so, so sorry
   for your loss.

Among giants, I carry my heart.

Geminis

My mother didn't understand herself.
I was born to a seventeen-year-old girl
who quit school to hide from the teacher
who wanted her to abort me.
The baby starts to kick,
you love it, you want it to be.
Her dark eyes focused on mine
when I came to her
from some place of mystery.
She tells it this way: I didn't know
what I was doing, only that I loved you.

*

She came into my room at night
to make sure I was breathing
I caught her once, a finger under my nose
she laughed and said *just checking*
leaving into the lighted hallway

*

My mother on the white, cordless phone
bare feet wrapped behind her legs
My mother's dark bangs cut above her dark eyes
My mother's youth   mid thirties

Her right shoulder lifted to her chin when she makes a joke
Her hands raised in church, beyond the ceiling tiles
Her faith holding the rest of us to heaven.

*

I remember that girl   /   her little book

the top bunk   looking out the tapered window

I feel her hopelessness
if she would just stop—

everything is so romantic

*

Please don't be normal.
Please don't pull your hand back inside.
Let the rain darken your dry skin
Please.
Let this message reach you
beyond the window
you sneak from
grass like freedom,
Little Girl,
please,
let it also touch your hair.

A month after the accident
General Motors representatives came to the door
we need the car
they said to my mother
What?   (It was completely destroyed)
What are you saying
What they're trying to tell us
without *actually* telling us
is that they know what happened
there's a dark cloak over the file cabinet in their office
we need you to hide inside it
we need you to wear this
these GM stock dollars
around your mouth.

I can't breathe with you in the room. You suck out the air when your briefcase opens and leaves a cross-examined witness tongue tied. I still know people who think my stepfather killed himself and murdered the kids. How does a man go without justice, the honor of his good name?

No, you may not have my silence.

I know what you're doing. You're becoming a moth. I see you
in the light, eating human fabric, building your wings.
I can hear your hum in the courtroom,
your veracious plea to Congress, spreading the disease
of supply and demand, ordering faulty parts: production, production!
Where is my family now? Can you tell me?
I saw smoke rise to the sky
and still do not know. They earned their place among the innocent
whose blood cries out from the earth   for justice.

I keep looking
        for the last thing
the song played in the car   the last time you were with me
            where we drove
            the last time
I brought lunch for you at work

On my way to Austin
            at the window   after an argument
        the last time   you laughed it off
I was home
            I watched the kids
            the last time
    we were whole.

In the abyss
        I close my eyes
        and shiver—

turn my
head
away from
nothing.

I Heard My Brother's Voice

Nothing actually separates. Life is a mirror,
a shadow of another side. My loved ones
walk with me to school, let me feel them
enter a room. It's not just the crosses on
the side of the road, or balloons we send
to reach them. I heard my brother's voice
lying in the garden.

I know they didn't die, but it's absence
that bothers me. I forget that I helped
my mother raise five children.
As the oldest, you subscribe naturally
to motherhood. I held their hand
across the street, fastened their belts
in the car, taught them to kick their legs
back to move the swing.

I see the world spin when I press into it,
a sundial making its way around.
I've heard every eternal verse, drank
its nourishment. I'm no longer hungry
in the place I buried my family,
I'm moved by force to gather fragments,
watch them glimmer with light from inside.

Origins of Healing

You know you're changing
when a vision in the sun is more real

    than the death that caused it.

It brought me to it, the sun.
It beckoned *me*.
The grasses lay gently underneath

    shaping my body.

I feel the world turn slightly.
The sun casts shadows,

    a rose shape.

I couldn't tell you about the accident
if it didn't happen. How I felt god or how
his voice weakened my body and I could only
lie down on the carpet.
I dealt with the shaking, learned to calm
the tremors like someone smoothing their hair
brushing out tangles with a comb.
Sometimes I recognize grief so much
I can't focus. I wear it like a bear
around my shoulders, its claws clasped at
my throat   I told you I loved you, I tried to tell you.
In the grass   I was once   a resident
in your time of grief, I won't interject
I won't tell you it's time to move on
I won't hang the phone up while you speak
I won't.

PJ, will you write a poem for the funeral?

The New Beatitudes

When I wear the dress at my knees
    and it spins
    the wind catches
adrift in the sound   of clouds passing through fibers
blue is the preface   to mourning
    the sky's hand against your shoulder

    lovely is the skin of those   who cry
      who were picked up in their grandmother's yard
    brought into the house
unable to use her legs
 We were falling apart.
    Performing ballet in the grass.
I hardly remember what was said   just those damn blue skies
    unfit weather for car accidents   too beautiful
to blame it on rain.

Happiness Is

A small blue pill
in the morning.
I rise to not need
      wholeness.
If I allow brain stems to regrow in the night
Into the brightness of light matter
It can dispel thoughts that come in from the shadow
Take inventory   transferring frequencies
Shield my brain from untruths
Those combative phrases about self
Thought life of one who is a series
Of fragments   glass shards broken into the grass
What is reformation? It stands attention to my tongue
It stands attention when I say *arise*
Arise and raise your hands in praise
To the universe inside you
The sun's reflection   on its stars.

The months before the baby comes are oddly still.
For now   it's just a lump growing in my belly   the same life
I savor this   as I savor all lasts
when great change seeks me out
altering the existence I know
 I am humbly quiet   lying in bed with the windows open.

This is my path   my song   I will carry this cadence into other rooms
 there are never days
I wish away the weight   the burden of what it is I must do
                                        I will speak to you
follow my voice into the hallway.

I find comfort in something
                because I am human.
    Wax grown on the outside of the grass blade
                doesn't make it resistant
                to April's springtime worm.
I am growing hydrangeas.
This time next year they will bloom
pastel pom-poms
beneath the window sill.
I look forward to it
                and what else may be different
in the garden.

The older I get   the less I find wholeness in anything
flowers blossom with missing petals   someone walks by
ripping them up.
I can't find comfort in delayed justice

                but a cedar grows on the plowed field anyway.

www.ingramcontent.com/pod-product-compliance
Lightning Source LLC
Chambersburg PA
CBHW060420050426
42449CB00009B/2054